The
Survivor's
Guide

Dedication

To my parents Dick and Sharon,
brother William, and husband Ted
for all of your love and support.

To Les Johnson for being there,
and for believing in me.
I couldn't have done it without you.

Special thanks to Dr. Steve Royce
of the University of Portland
for all of his valued assistance
in the creation of this book and
for having the endurance
to see this project to the end.

Special thanks to Charity Harding
for all of her helpful feedback,
and to Gretchen Kathleen Brokamp
for her responses to the cover design.

Also thanks to all of the young women
in my groups who have taught me so much.

The Survivor's Guide

Sharice A. Lee

SAGE Publications
International Educational and Professional Publisher
Thousand Oaks   London   New Delhi

For information address:

 SAGE Publications, Inc.
2455 Teller Road
Thousand Oaks, California 91320
E-mail: order@sagepub.com

SAGE Publications Ltd.
6 Bonhill Street
London EC2A 4PU
United Kingdom

SAGE Publications India Pvt. Ltd.
M-32 Market
Greater Kailash I
New Delhi 110 048 India

Printed in the United States of America

Library of Congress Cataloging-in-Publication Data

Lee, Sharice A.
    The survivor's guide: For teenage girls surviving sexual
abuse / Sharice A. Lee.
        p.   cm.
    ISBN 0-8039-5780-7 (cl.: acid-free paper). — ISBN 0-8039-5781-5 (pbk.)
    1. Teenage sexual abuse victims—United States—Case studies.
    2. Teenage sexual abuse victims—Mental health—United States—
    Case studies.   I. Title.
    HV6570.2.L44   1995
    362.7'64'0973—dc20   94-45028

This book is printed on acid-free paper.

00   13 12 11 10 9 8 7

Production Editor: Yvonne Könneker
Ventura Typesetter: Janelle LeMaster

Contents

Beginnings

Being a victim of sexual abuse is not easy. It can make a person feel confused, ashamed, and all kinds of other things. This book tries to clear up some of the confusion by providing information to survivors of sexual abuse about how the abuse can affect a person. If you are a survivor of abuse, you should know that these effects are from the sexual abuse, not from you. It is not because you are bad, it is because what happened to you is bad and the people who abused you should not have done those things to you.

All the examples in this book are real. Sometimes reading these examples can bring up memories of your own abuse and those memories can be hard to deal with. Because it could bring up your own abuse memories, it's best to read this book when you are around people you trust who you can talk to about the abuse if you need to. If lots of abuse memories start to come up and it's hard to deal with, you may want to slow down your reading a bit. Perhaps read one chapter each week or take it even slower if you need to. If you read anything that you don't understand, or find something that you want to know more about, be sure and ask an adult whom you trust about it so that you can get the information you need.

In this book, it is mentioned over and over that it can be very helpful to talk to people you trust about the abuse. Talking about the abuse takes some of its power away and makes it so that you're not dealing with all of the emotions and confusion by yourself anymore. It is best if you have both adults and people your own age whom you trust and can talk to about the abuse. You are probably around the people your own age the most often, so they can usually be there for you more than the adults. Adults, especially counselors, are more likely to know how to help you, or at least know how to get you that help. If you start talking to some people about the abuse, and they have trouble understanding, try using the book to help them understand. Ask them to read the sections of the book that might help them better understand what it's like for you, and then talk to them some more. The effects of abuse can be pretty confusing, and sometimes it takes more than just talking to understand.

While reading this book, it's very important to respect where you're at in being ready to deal with the abuse. It's OK to give yourself time. It takes years for some survivors to be able to tell people that the abuse happened, and it may take even longer to feel ready to get some help coping with what happened. For example, Kelly was molested when she was 5, but she was so afraid that people would think it was all her fault, she didn't tell a single soul until she was 32 years old. She felt better after she told someone, but it was another whole year before she felt ready to get counseling. Abuse is a tough thing to cope with and no one should have to do it alone. Getting counseling means having someone on your side to listen and help clear up some of the confusion and problems abuse can cause. You may not be ready, willing, or able to get counseling at this time, but when you are ready and able, getting help can make things a lot easier.

Triggers

A *trigger* is anything that reminds you of the abuse; it's anything that brings up memories of what happened to you. A trigger can be just about anything: a smell, a sound, a touch, or something you see. Smelling the cologne that the offender wore, seeing a couch like the one you were abused on, or hearing some music that you heard when you were being abused are all examples of things that could be triggers. Being triggered is normal for someone who has had something very hurtful happen to her, and sexual abuse is a very hurtful thing.

The following is an example of an abuse survivor who was triggered by a certain kind of touch. After school, Chrissy meets a bunch of her friends over at Jim's house to watch a movie. During a break in the movie, everyone starts goofing around. Chrissy reaches over and starts tickling her friend Jim. Laughing hysterically, Jim grabs Chrissy's wrists and pins her to the floor to keep her from tickling him more. Getting her wrists pinned to the floor is a trigger for Chrissy because it reminds her of how her offender used to pin her wrists to the floor while he raped her. Chrissy starts to feel really scared even though she knows Jim would never hurt her. Chrissy yells at Jim to let go of her, then she locks herself in the bathroom and cries because being triggered has brought up memories of being raped and all the bad feelings that went with it.

This next example tells about a girl who is triggered by certain things people say to her. Misty was sexually abused by her brother Jay when she was 7 years old. Jay always used to tell her that he never would have had sex with her if it wasn't for the fact that she was so pretty. He used to tell her that she was so pretty he just couldn't help himself around her, and then he would molest her. Misty is 15 now, and whenever a guy tells her she is pretty, Misty feels uncomfortable around him and kind of afraid. Being told she is pretty is a trigger for Misty because it's something she was told by her offender every time she was molested by him.

Specific places can also be triggers. Sara was sexually abused at her uncle's house by her cousin David. David doesn't live at the house anymore, but Sara still feels afraid every time she visits there. Every time Sara sees her uncle's house, she gets pictures in her head of being molested there. The house is a trigger for Sara. People tend to associate places with past events that took place there, which is why memories are triggered. For example, if you have had fun at a particular park in the past and you go back to that park, you will probably think of the good times you have had there and feel happy and good. If you have been abused there, you will probably feel afraid and bad.

There are virtually hundreds of ways a person can be triggered. The examples above

cover just a few, and you will find more examples of triggers throughout this book.

To summarize, a trigger is something that
causes you to remember the abuse in some
way.

Panic attacks, intrusive memories, and flashbacks are all things that can happen after a
person has been triggered. In the next couple
of sections in this book, these three things will
be explained.

Panic Attacks

When a person is triggered, one thing that can happen is something called a *panic attack*. A panic attack is your body reacting to the abuse trigger, and it usually involves feeling very afraid or upset. The following is a list of the things a person might experience during a panic attack:

Suddenly feeling afraid or nervous
Hypervigilance/feel paranoid or jumpy
Adrenaline rush
Trembling or shaking
Difficulty thinking or concentrating

Sweaty hands or getting sweaty all over
A powerful urge to run or "get out of here"
Upset stomach/feel like you have to throw up
Feeling numb
Heart beats fast
Hot flashes or chills
Feeling out of control
Dissociation/"spacing out"
Feeling afraid to move
Suddenly start crying or sudden urge to cry
Difficulty understanding words people say
Hyperventilating/trouble breathing
Feeling confused
Having trouble getting words out of your mouth
Feeling shaky or faint
Feeling like things are unreal or in a dream

Some panic attacks involve just a few of these symptoms, and others include almost the whole list. When a panic attack happens, the person having it usually doesn't know what triggered the panic attack right away. This is because when a person is triggered, her brain perceives the situation as dangerous and often tries to move her away from the danger mentally and emotionally.

For example, Diane was raped by her brother's friend Shawn. One day Diane was hanging out with friends at the mall when she hears someone talking about Shawn. Hearing the name of the guy who raped her triggers Diane. Diane's heart starts beating fast, her hands get sweaty, she feels afraid, and her stomach hurts like she's going to throw up. At first Diane feels terrified; she doesn't know why things feel so out of control. Soon she realizes that she is having a panic attack and tries to calm herself down by remembering her friends' promise never to let Shawn near her again.

Here is another example of a panic attack with some different symptoms. Jamie was sexually abused 4 years ago. No one ever taught Jamie about triggers or panic attacks, but every time Jamie hears someone talking about sexual abuse she feels like running away and crying. All of a sudden everything seems like it's a dream and she feels confused and scared. Jamie doesn't know it, but whenever she hears someone talk about sexual abuse it triggers her, and those strange feelings she has are part of a panic attack.

Panic attacks and triggers almost always go together. It takes time to identify what your own personal triggers are, but once you do, panic attacks tend to become less frightening. Both dealing with the abuse in counseling, instead of just pretending it never happened, and the passage of time are things that help make panic attacks less severe.

Flashbacks and Intrusive Memories

A *flashback* is a type of memory that is so strong it seems like you are actually back in the time, place, and situation you are remembering. An *intrusive memory* is simply having a memory of your abuse that pops into your head all of a sudden. Both flashbacks and intrusive memories are often caused by being triggered. For example, an intensive memory could be triggered by hearing other survivors talk about the details of their abuse. As another example, a flashback could be triggered by trying to remember a specific detail about the abuse, like a survivor trying to remember exactly what her offender said to her when he tried to get her to unzip his pants.

Both flashbacks and intrusive memories cause you to get pictures in your head of what happened. Sometimes the people and things in the pictures stand still like they are frozen in time or like someone took pictures of them with a camera. Sometimes the people and things in the pictures move, just like you are watching a movie on television. In a flashback/intrusive memory, you might see just one picture or you might see the whole movie.

The difference between a flashback and an intrusive memory is simple: In an intrusive memory, all you get are pictures in your head. In a flashback, you have the pictures in your head, and it seems like the abuse is happening to you all over again. In a flashback, it is even possible to smell smells, hear sounds, and feel touch.

During flashbacks, sometimes your body remembers what the abuse felt like when it was happening to you. Emotions also are sometimes remembered during flashbacks. If you were feeling really scared and upset when you were being abused, the flashback might make you feel the same way again. If you felt numb when you got abused, you might feel numb when you get flashbacks.

Flashbacks can be really scary. When someone is in the middle of a flashback, it's easy to lose track of what is going on in the real world outside of the flashback. It can be really hard to understand what people are saying to you when you are in a flashback. Some flashbacks are so confusing it gets hard to tell the difference between what is happening in the flashback and what is happening in the real world.

The following is an example of a flashback. Mandy gets a ride home from soccer practice with her friend Tina. On the way home, they pick up Tina's 7-year-old sister. The sister has on a red sweater just like the one Mandy had when she was that age. Mandy smiles as she remembers what she looked like wearing that sweater when she was small. All of a sudden, Mandy's smile turns into a frown as she sees her offender come into the picture in her head. Mandy realizes that her offender molested her when she was wearing that sweater one Fourth of July.

Mandy starts having a flashback. She feels really afraid, and in her head she sees her offender sitting on the bed in front of her, telling her to put her arms up as he slips the sweater off of her. She sees him throw the sweater into the corner of her bedroom. She remembers just staring at the sweater in the corner while he takes the rest of her clothes off. Mandy starts feeling cold like she always did after her offender took her clothes off. Being in the flashback, it's almost like she can feel his big, sweaty hands on her skin.

Mandy feels terrified because she knows what her offender is going to do to her. Back in the real world, outside of the pictures in her head, Mandy can see her friend talking to her, but she has no idea what Tina is saying to her because she is still in the flashback. Mandy tries to at least act like she is listening to her friend. Mandy feels confused; she knows that the abuse couldn't be happening again, but it all seems so real. She tries hard to make it all go away, but it doesn't work. She hears her offender's heavy breathing, and then he tells her how good it feels to have sex with her. Mandy just keeps hearing and seeing and feeling the whole thing. She decides she will just try to stay calm and hang on until it all goes away.

Having a flashback is a very frightening experience. It can be just as frightening as actually being abused. Intrusive memories can also be scary and upsetting but usually aren't as bad as flashbacks. What follows is an example of an intrusive memory. Faith was at home thinking about the homework she had to get done that night when she heard a story come on the TV about prostitution. All of a sudden, Faith's mind was full of pictures of Mike, the guy who molested her, telling her that she had to have sex with this friend of his because he had paid $50 for her. Remembering this part of her abuse, Faith felt upset, ashamed, and sick to her stomach. Being molested by a guy who had paid money for her made her feel so gross and icky. Faith hated thinking about this kind of stuff; she just wished that it would pop out of her head as quickly as it had popped in.

Flashbacks and intrusive memories are tough to deal with, and unfortunately, there is no magic cure for either of them. Many survivors find that if they stick to their counseling, the flashbacks and memories don't happen as often, and when they do happen, they aren't as scary or upsetting as they were in the past.

Because most survivors are used to keeping everything about their abuse a secret, when flashbacks or memories or fears about the abuse come up, they tend to keep those a secret too. For example, Gina is riding in the car with Alan, the person she trusts the most in the world, when a song on the radio triggers an abuse memory that is really scary for her. Even though she feels really upset and scared, Gina doesn't even think of telling Alan about how she's feeling because she's just not used to talking about things like that. Thanks to the abuse, Gina is used to acting normal on the outside even though she is freaking out on the inside. Even though Gina puts on a great act that everything is fine, Alan notices that she is quieter than normal and asks her what's wrong. Gina tells him, "Nothing, I'm just tired."

If you have flashbacks or abuse memories and you keep them a secret from the people you trust, you may be depriving yourself of a lot of caring and support from those people. One thing you can do about flashbacks and memories with or without counseling is tell the people you trust how they can help when you are going through a flashback or a memory. Then give them the opportunity to help by letting them in on the secret and telling them when you're having a memory or flashback. Does it help if they give you a hug, or does it feel better if they stay a few feet away? Do you feel safer if they talk to you, or do you prefer they just be there for you without saying anything? Even little pieces of information like these can make your friends feel good because you're trusting them enough to let them help. Letting friends help can make you feel like you don't have to deal with it all alone and make the whole thing easier to handle. Letting some people you trust in on the secret and letting others help you can make things better for everyone.

Bad Dreams

It is normal for survivors of sexual abuse to have bad dreams about what happened to them. Many survivors have nightmares that their offenders come back and hurt them, or they dream they are getting abused again. The defenses that we normally put up to help us keep from thinking about our abuse during the day go down at night when we go to sleep. Because our defenses are down when we are asleep, it is easier for scary thoughts to creep into our heads.

If you have bad dreams almost every night, you might be so scared of having bad dreams that you can't go to sleep. Not being able to sleep is very stressful and can cause problems in your life. If you have bad dreams about the abuse, it often helps to talk about the dreams with a counselor or someone you trust. Having bad dreams is a normal part of healing from abuse. Healing takes time, and it will take time for the bad dreams to go away too.

Memory Gaps

It is common for trauma survivors to have what is known as *memory gaps*. These are blank spots in a person's memory. Some survivors remember none of their abuse at all, some remember just a little bit of the abuse, some remember most of their abuse but still have a few pieces missing, and others have no memory of entire years of their lives.

Just because you can't remember some of the things that happened to you doesn't mean that these things are gone from your brain forever. It simply means that the memories of those events are "hidden" in a part of your brain that you don't have access to right now. It's kind of like a computer program that you have to have an access code to get into or a door you can't open unless you have a key.

Your brain keeps these events a "secret" from you to protect you from feeling more hurt than you can handle. Most of the time, when your brain "decides" that you are emotionally ready, it will slowly begin to let you remember the memories it has been protecting you from.

When memory begins to come back, the brain usually just gives you bits and pieces or small flashes of the memory at first, and the pictures may be a bit fuzzy at the beginning. Eventually, the pieces begin to fit together like a jigsaw puzzle, and you are finally able to remember the whole thing. Sometimes memories come back so slowly and fuzzy that you might be unsure whether it is a real memory or just a dream. If you have memory gaps, do not try to force yourself to remember; the memory will come back to you in time. The memory gaps are just a way of protecting yourself.

The brain's protection system is, unfortunately, far from perfect. Sometimes, something will come along that really reminds your memory banks of the abuse; this is known as a trigger. If a strong enough trigger comes along, it can punch a hole in your brain's security system and cause a memory to come up before you are ready for it. Having a memory before you are ready for it can be a stressful, scary situation and might even bring on a panic attack or flashback. If this ever happens to you, it is very important that you take action to get some help and support in order to keep yourself safe. Don't get down on yourself for having a hard time coping; it's to be expected that it will be difficult.

It is important to understand that even though you may have hidden memories that you aren't aware of right now, a part of your brain is aware of them and does know about them, so they can still affect you and cause problems for you. Having memory gaps is kind of like having a complicated jigsaw puzzle with some pieces missing. If lots of the pieces are missing, it can make the puzzle pretty confusing. If you have memory gaps, and some things about your abuse seem confusing, just remember that the confusion is normal.

Self-Harm

Self-harm is doing damage to, or hurting, your own body on purpose. Many survivors of sexual abuse use self-harm as a way of dealing with the pain and emotions caused by their abuse. The most common forms of self-harm are cutting and burning, but other methods are sometimes used.

There are a lot of reasons why survivors hurt themselves. Sexual abuse is an awful thing to have to go through. Even when it isn't happening at the moment, in a way, the abuse stays with you. The feelings and the fear and the memories are still there. It's hard to deal with, and it's hard to talk about. Sometimes it can feel like all the awful feelings and memories from the abuse have invaded your whole body and not just your mind. For some victims, cutting on themselves feels like actually cutting all of the feelings and bad memories out of their bodies. So some victims cut on themselves to try to get rid of all the bad memories and feelings caused by the abuse.

To some victims, hurting their bodies is a way of doing something with their anger. Instead of hurting the person she is angry at, the victim hurts herself. She turns her anger in toward herself instead of out toward the person she is mad at. For example, Joni feels extremely mad at Tom, the guy who abused her, because she just found out that he also abused her best friend. Joni is so angry she wants to hurt Tom, but she knows if she tries he will end up hurting her worse. In the past, anytime Joni showed anger toward Tom, he beat her up. Still, Joni is so angry she has to do something with it, so she takes it out on herself. Joni cuts on herself and pretends she is stabbing Tom. Hurting herself is Joni's way of getting out the intense anger she feels.

Some survivors use self-harm to try to gain control when they are feeling emotional pain. It is sometimes hard to figure out where emotional pain is coming from, and it's also a hard thing to control. If you hurt yourself, at least you know where this pain is coming from, and you are controlling it. You control how much, how often, and what kind. Sometimes, physical pain can distract you from intense emotional pain by taking your mind off it. The physical hurt becomes the focus of your attention, helping you to get away from the emotional hurt a bit.

When the human body gets really hurt, it releases a group of chemicals called *endorphins*. Endorphins are a lot like narcotics chemically, and they have some of the same effects. When endorphins are released in the body, the person feels a "rush" similar to the rush a person might feel after shooting heroin into the veins. Some people hurt their bodies because this rush, along with other effects of these chemicals, gets their minds off the emotional pain or makes the emotional pain seem not so bad.

Endorphins, like narcotics, kill pain. The emotional pain, and sometimes even the physical pain, of sexual abuse can be really bad. When a human feels pain, the first instinct is to do something to make the pain go away. The pain from the abuse is often a lot worse than the pain from a cut or burn because it's deep emotional pain. The endorphins kill pain and help make the person numb. Being numb can feel very safe to a person who has had her body hurt by other people against her will.

If someone were to cut your body with a knife, you could see the wound; you could even touch it and see it bleed. Things we can see with our eyes somehow seem more real than things we can't see or touch. Other people could see the wound too. They could see that you got hurt and know that you are feeling pain. Emotional wounds are not so easy to see. They tend to stay hidden deep inside us where no one can see that we got hurt and no one knows that we are feeling this pain. Perhaps no one tries to help you with your wounds inside because they can't see them, because they don't know that the wounds are there. It is hard for people to help you deal with the abuse or give you support if no one knows you have been abused. That is one reason why it is important to tell people you trust about it. Once they know, they can give you help and support.

For example, Alisha is hanging out at a friend's house when memories of her abuse take over her head. Thinking about all of the things her offender did to her really hurts. The hurt keeps running through her head and her body, and it seems to be getting worse. She can't stop thinking about it. Alisha feels like crying or screaming or doing anything to make it go away, but it won't go away. She feels trapped, like there is no way she can escape the hurt. Alisha wants someone to help her get through this and be there for her, but none of her friends seem to notice that she is hurting. Even if her friends did notice, she couldn't tell them how to help her because she doesn't know what kind of help she needs. Alisha feels so confused, she doesn't know what to do.

Alisha goes into the bathroom, takes out her knife, and starts cutting her arm with it. It hurts at first, but at least she can see where this pain is coming from, and she knows how to make this pain stop if she wants. After she cuts, she feels a rush that pushes the memories and feelings out for a minute or two. When the rush is over, the memories and feelings come back, but they aren't so bad this time. Alisha doesn't feel so hurt, she just feels kind of numb. She finds herself staring at the reflection of the light off the blade of her knife and the blood seeping out of her arm; the memories in her head don't seem so overwhelming any more. When Alisha comes out of the bathroom, her friends notice her wound right away. Alisha's friends rush over to help her, getting bandages and asking her what is wrong. With this kind of hurt, Alisha doesn't even need to ask for help let alone try to tell everyone how to help her. This kind of pain is sure a lot simpler to deal with!

Even though you may feel confused and not know what kind of help to ask for, or even if it seems like people won't understand, it's important to tell someone you trust about what happened and when you are feeling hurt about it. This stuff is always hard to talk about, but really the only way that other people can see an emotional wound is if you show it to them by telling them what happened and how it has made you feel. There are external signs of emotional wounds, but they are much more difficult to see than the signs of physical wounds. So sometimes you have to help people see them, just like a microscope helps a doctor see a germ that is making your body sick.

Self-harm is a coping mechanism that many survivors use to deal with the emotional pain of sexual abuse. Because it causes damage to the survivor's body it is a dangerous coping mechanism. It is important to learn different ways of dealing with the pain so that you can keep yourself safe. All survivors deserve to be safe.

Drugs and Alcohol

Drugs and alcohol are another way some abuse survivors try to deal with the bad memories and feelings from their abuse. They use drugs to make the memories and feelings go away or to try to gain control over them temporarily. A person who is feeling depressed and upset over her abuse might take a stimulant to try to make herself feel better. A survivor having a panic attack might take a tranquilizer to calm herself down. A person who has been having nightmares about her abuse decides to take a depressant to knock herself out at night so she won't dream. A survivor who feels bad about herself snorts cocaine to feel more likable or shoots crank to gain control of her overeating. She might have a few drinks before going out for the evening to help her feel less nervous and jumpy around crowds, or she might take a pill to try to keep the bad memories away.

It is obvious that drugs and alcohol are very appealing to the abuse survivor because they can make some of the bad effects of sexual abuse go away for a while. For a survivor who uses chemicals in an attempt to deal with her abuse, it is easy to become addicted very quickly. The effects of the chemicals only last for a short time, so she must keep using the chemicals over and over to keep covering up the effects of the sexual abuse. She must use them almost all the time to maintain the "imitation stability" they provide.

For every good thing about chemical use, there is a bad thing about it that shoots the good thing down. When a person does drugs on a regular basis, much of her money goes in her mouth, up her nose, or in her veins. Then, when the money runs out, the addict may find herself doing things she is not proud of to get the drugs she needs.

Drug and alcohol use are hard on the body. Spending the night on the bathroom floor throwing up, a nose that won't stop running, brain drain, early morning hangovers, cotton mouth, eyes that are red and sore, veins that an ice pick couldn't penetrate, tweaking, crashing, and coming down hard are just a few of the "thrills" they offer.

And let's not forget dealers who always want money, hassles with the law, meth monsters at midnight, and crank cooties at dawn. How about crashing your car because you were so wasted you forgot to steer, worrying over how you are going to get more drugs before you come down, or not being able to remember where you were or what you did last night and then finding out you were out making a fool out of yourself in front of just about everyone you know. Losing someone you care about to drugs or alcohol. Losing yourself. Sometimes drugs can make you feel awfully good, and a second later they can hurt you awfully bad. As a survivor you have been hurt enough, and if you use drugs and alcohol, you will be hurt some more.

The survivor/addict must deal with both the abuse and the addiction. Because the two problems have been so tangled up, one will not go away unless the other is dealt with. Using drugs and alcohol to get rid of the hurt and bad memories of sexual abuse for a while can seem like the only way to survive. It might seem like an act of self-preservation or self-medication to the survivor. In reality, however, it is very self-destructive because it keeps dragging you closer and closer to physical harm and death. It is like death disguised as a savior. Don't be fooled by the disguise.

Power and Control

When a person is sexually abused, the offender takes control of the victim and her body by forcing sex on her against her will. He has almost complete power over her, and he uses it to harm her. The victim learns that not having power and control can mean danger and hurt; it doesn't feel safe. She learns that letting others have power and control over her can make it easier for others to hurt her. After being abused, the survivor often feels unsafe in any situation in which she believes she doesn't have power and control. Therefore, she may try to stay away from these situations or try to gain control in whatever way she can. As a result, survivors often become very good at controlling the people and situations around them.

Some of the "tools" survivors use to control people and situations include:

Lying
Secrets
Anger/aggression
Sex and seduction
Playing people against each other
Trying to make others dependent on you
Planting guilt trips/blaming others
Making fools of others/setting people up
Withholding information
Starting rumors
Making threats/blackmail
Playing victim/encouraging sympathy
Using money, status, drugs, or material things

Using tools such as these to control others can affect a person's life in negative ways. These ways of manipulating are a part of relationships that are dishonest and sneaky. It is hard to get any love and support from relationships in which you can't really trust each other. Nervousness and stress are two other negative effects of trying to manipulate others. If you're always busy trying to control the puppets, it's pretty hard to sit back and enjoy the puppet show.

The need to feel in control may cause a person to try to get around the rules much of the time. She may have the attitude that "rules were made to be broken" to prove to herself that the rules don't control her, she can do what she wants, and she is in control. This type of attitude can lead to criminal behavior, problems with the law, and trouble getting along with authority figures.

Using manipulative ways to control people usually works pretty well at first, but as time goes on the use of these methods starts rapidly taking power and control out of the user's hands. For example, let's say Jenny tells a lie to her probation officer to avoid going to detention. By lying, which is a way of manipulating people, Jenny gets some control over the situation for a little while, but not for long. A friend of Jenny's named Ann finds out about the lie and starts blackmailing

Jenny. Jenny now has lost almost all of her power and control; she has to do whatever Ann tells her or go to detention even longer than she would have had to before because they will find out she lied. By using manipulation, Jenny has opened up the door for Ann to take control over her.

If you have a manipulative style of relating to others, it can keep you from having the type of friends who are honest and stay away from trouble. We tend to act like the people we hang out with. This is an excellent reason to get counseling if you want to be the type of person who stays out of trouble and who can be trusted.

Blaming Yourself

Guilt is one of the toughest emotions survivors have to deal with. Lots of abuse survivors feel guilty because they believe it was their fault that they got sexually abused. They blame themselves for what happened to them.

Most of us would like to believe that we live in a world that is basically safe, most people are trustworthy and good, and we have control over what happens to us. If we admit that the abuse wasn't our fault, we also have to admit that the world isn't very safe and that we don't always have control. If we don't have control, that means we could be sexually assaulted again no matter what we do to try to prevent it—a very scary thing to accept.

For example, Tami believes that if she hadn't been so stupid and gone out of her bedroom in her nightgown, her dad never would have had sex with her. She decides that as long as she never comes out of her room in her nightgown again, she won't make her dad get turned on and he won't do that to her anymore. Then she can feel safe. If Tami admitted to herself that her dad was to blame for raping her and that she and her nightgown had nothing to do with his actions, then she would have to accept the fact that someone might do that to her again even if she never, ever wears a nightgown in front of him again.

Thinking that it could happen again no matter what she does is just too scary for Tami. So Tami decides to believe that it was her fault and that she can keep the abuse from happening again as long as she doesn't wear any more nightgowns. Many of us are like Tami; we don't want to admit that sometimes we don't have any control and that people can hurt us even if we try really hard to stay safe. Blaming the abuse on something we did or said, a certain way we were acting, or the way we were dressed are all ways of convincing ourselves that we were in control of what happened; we caused the offender to do what he did. Of course we didn't cause the abuse, but for many of us, feeling guilty because we believe it was our fault is better than feeling powerless because we believe it was the offender's fault. Feeling powerless seems just too frightening.

Another reason people who have been sexually abused blame themselves is something called the *broken-record principle*. The broken-record principle says that if you hear the same thing over and over lots of times, you will probably start to believe what you have been hearing even if it's not true. Sometimes these "broken records" are things we tell ourselves, and sometimes they are things other people tell us.

Christy's story is a good example of the broken-record principle. For years, Christy has been telling herself that getting raped was her own fault. After all, she did smile at him. She figures that must have made him think she wanted it. So every time she starts to feel upset about getting raped she tells herself, "I shouldn't feel upset, it was my fault." Of course it wasn't Christy's fault, and she has a right to feel upset, but her own broken record is telling her something different.

Lori's offender always tells her that the only reason he has sex with her is because he can tell she wants it. Lori knows she doesn't want sex, but after a while she starts to believe what her offender tells her because he has told her that so many times. She gives in to her offender's broken record and starts to believe that she does want to have sex with him, ignoring her real feelings of fear and shame. Besides, it's nicer to believe that she wants sex with her offender because that would mean that she's getting what she wants, which is much easier to accept than the truth. The truth is that sex is being forced on her against her will.

Most people would agree that there is no such thing as a person who is always 100% good or 100% bad. The person who sexually abused you may have been really mean and hurtful while abusing you but really nice and helpful at other times. Some survivors feel guilty for getting upset at their offender for abusing them when he is so good to them the rest of the time. A survivor may even feel like she owes her offender sex because of all he does for her or all of the stuff he buys for her. For example, Tasha's offender is like the father she never had. He helps her with her homework, takes her out to dinner every week, gives her money for clothes, and tells her how terrific she is whenever she feels down. Sometimes after her offender has sexually abused her, Tasha feels like she hates him. Then later, she feels guilty for hating him because he is so nice to her most of the time. Tasha thinks to herself, "How can I be so upset about this. I owe it to him after he spent $200 on me for new clothes. I should just learn to take it without getting upset." Tasha needs to understand that it is OK to feel hate for someone who has sexually abused you but to still like some of the nice things he has done for you. It would also help Tasha to learn that she does not owe her offender sex no matter how much money he chooses to spend on her.

In the above example, Tasha felt guilty for hating her offender after he has done so many nice things for her. Some victims of sexual assault have just the opposite problem; they feel guilty because they still like their offender, or sometimes even feel like they love him, while friends and family say they should hate his guts. For example, let's say Tasha still likes her offender even though he abused her because he also did lots of nice things for her. When Tasha tells her family that she misses her offender sometimes, they tell Tasha she must either be crazy or must have liked having sex with him if she misses him after what he did to her. Tasha feels guilty and tells herself, "I must be pretty stupid to miss the guy who used to rape me; I'm a total slut." Tasha is not stupid, crazy, or a slut. It's common for people to still have some positive feelings about their offender, especially if they knew him awhile before he started to abuse them and they had some positive feelings about him then. Those positive feelings sometimes stick around despite the abuse, and it's not wrong to have those feelings.

Abuse survivors sometimes feel guilty if their offenders get in trouble for sexually abusing them. For example, Julie's offender gets put in jail for sexually abusing her. Julie is glad he is gone so he can't abuse her anymore, but she feels bad for "getting him in trouble." It's important for Julie to realize that she isn't responsible for getting her offender in trouble; he got himself in trouble by doing something against the law. Julie's offender got in trouble for what *he did* not for what she said.

Being sexually abused is a terrible thing to have to go through. Sometimes family and friends get upset when they find out about the sexual abuse. Families are sometimes separated due to sexual abuse, and this can also cause people to get upset. If these things happen, the abuse victim might feel guilty and blame herself for the upset feelings of friends and family. Sometimes the friends and family also blame the victim for their upset feelings and other problems caused by the sexual abuse because they are too afraid to blame the person who is at fault, the offender. It is really sad that the victim sometimes gets blamed for things that are not her fault.

Getting over feeling guilty and coming to believe that the abuse was not your fault is a process that takes time. It may help to use the broken-record principle in a positive way. Every time you think of the abuse tell yourself, "It wasn't my fault" and remind yourself that the offender was the one who broke the law and caused the problems, not you. Ask for support from people you trust if you need it and don't take the rap for something that isn't your fault! Remember that you did nothing wrong. He committed a crime against you and you are the one who was hurt.

Damaged-Goods Syndrome

Damaged-goods syndrome is the name given to a set of feelings, attitudes, and beliefs held by many victims about themselves. A person with damaged- goods syndrome often believes that because she was sexually abused, she is unclean or dirty and there is something bad about her body. The victim might believe that if people find out she was sexually abused, they will think she is bad and dirty and won't want to come near her or touch her.

These beliefs sometimes appear to be true because when people find out that you were a victim of sexual assault, they may be afraid to touch you because they think it might upset you. They know that sexual assault involves hurtful touching, and they don't want to risk doing anything that might bring up bad memories, or cause you to feel afraid or upset. Because they don't know any better, these people unknowingly contribute to the belief system of damaged-goods syndrome. The survivor tells them she was sexually abused, they quit touching her thinking this will protect her from bad feelings, and the survivor takes this lack of touch as a form of rejection and proof that other people see her as being dirty and bad because she was sexually abused.

For example, Michelle believes that because her body had disgusting things done to it during the abuse, her body is disgusting, dirty, and bad (beliefs that are a part of damaged-goods syndrome). Michelle wants to tell Dan, her teacher, about her abuse so that he can understand why she has panic attacks sometimes, but she is afraid to tell him. Dan always gives Michelle a pat on the back when she does good on a math test. Michelle is afraid that if Dan finds out she has been sexually abused, he won't want to get near her anymore, let alone touch her, and Michelle likes a pat on the back every once in a while.

One day, Michelle decides to take a risk, and she tells Dan that she has been abused and explains to him about the panic attacks. Michelle felt good that she finally told Dan; he seemed very understanding and supportive, and he agreed to give her some space if it looked like she was having a panic attack. The next day, Michelle gets her math test back with a big 100% written at the top of the page but no pat on the back. Dan just tells her, "good job" and moves on, giving other students who got good scores a pat on the back. Michelle feels rejected and hurt and tells herself, "I never should have told Dan, now he thinks I'm gross and he probably won't ever touch me again unless he has industrial-strength gloves on or something."

Later, Dan notices that Michelle looks upset and asks her what is wrong. Michelle says, "I told you that I was abused and now you probably wouldn't touch me with a 10-foot pole because you think I'm gross." Dan explains that the only reason he didn't give Michelle the usual pat on the back was because he was afraid it might upset her, and now that he knows it doesn't bother her, she can have all the pats on the back she wants. Then he gives Michelle the nicest pat on the back she ever got, and Michelle doesn't feel bad anymore.

The truth is that being sexually abused does not make a person unclean, dirty, or bad. Many offenders like to make their victims believe these things because it helps keep the victim from telling, but these things are not true. Even though it's absolutely not true that being sexually abused makes a person dirty or bad, if the offender who molested you was good at convincing you of these things, it may take time for you to believe it in your heart that you aren't dirty or bad. It's really worth doing some work to change that belief.

Lying

Part of being a victim of sexual abuse is learning to keep secrets. Our offenders tell us we must do whatever it takes to keep the abuse a secret, which often means the victim must lie about things like why she is upset, where she got those bruises, and why she doesn't want to go somewhere with her offender. Offenders often frighten victims into keeping the abuse a secret by making us think that if the secret gets out, something awful will happen to us or the people we love. So we learn to watch what we do and say, being careful not to give even the smallest hint that we are being sexually abused because we are afraid of what might happen if the secret gets out.

Learning to keep the abuse a secret means learning to lie about how we feel and what is happening to us. Take Becky, for example. Becky is in math class at school when she remembers that her parents are going out tonight, and she will be left alone with Jon, her baby-sitter. Whenever Becky gets left alone with Jon, he makes her have sex with him. After remembering this, Becky can't get her mind back on her math. She just sits there remembering what happened the last time she was left with Jon and starts feeling upset and scared. The teacher comes up and asks Becky why she's not doing her math. Becky lies and tells her teacher she's not doing her math because she thinks it's stupid. Becky doesn't really think the math is stupid; if she were to tell the truth, she would tell her teacher that she is feeling really upset about something and is having a really hard time concentrating on her math.

After class, Becky meets her friend Jan in the cafeteria; she still can't get her mind off the abuse. Jan asks Becky how she's doing; Becky feels afraid and upset. She wants to tell Jan how she's really feeling and why, but she's afraid of what would happen if she let someone find out about the abuse, even her best friend, so she lies and says she's fine. When she's asked what she's doing tonight, Becky lies again and says she's going to a movie with her parents. Later, Jon forces Becky to have sex with him and then asks Becky if she likes what he did to her. Becky lies and tells him she likes it because she's afraid that Jon will beat her up if she tells him the truth that she hates it.

Sexual abuse can affect a person's life in many ways; it's a big thing to try to keep secret. It takes a lot of lying and covering things up to keep a secret that big. For many victims, lying becomes a habit that is a part of their lives. They lie so much they hardly realize when they are doing it. The lies are like a wall that keeps people from seeing what is really inside.

Lying about how you feel and what is really going on in your life can isolate you from others and cause you to feel lonely. Lying prevents other people from getting to know the real you, and if no one can get to know the real you, that means the real you is all alone. The lies keep you from feeling real love and friendship.

The next example is a story to help show how lying forms a wall between yourself and other people and keeps others from getting to know you. The metal robot costume in the story is like the wall that lying creates. Let's imagine Cindy goes to an expensive costume store and buys a giant metal robot costume. After she buys the costume, she wears it all the time and acts like a robot so that nobody knows there is a person inside. For a while, Cindy likes being a robot; she feels safe in her robot costume. When people put her down, it doesn't bother her because they are putting down the robot, not Cindy. She doesn't have to feel sad or ashamed or upset because robots don't feel those things. Cindy makes up all kinds of things about all of the neat places the robot has been and the great things it has done. She can invent its life story and make it as exciting and terrific as she wants. Cindy thinks this is much better than saying anything about her real life, which is depressing and doesn't seem as exciting as the stuff she's made up for the robot.

After a while, Cindy starts feeling lonely. She starts to realize that the robot has lots of friends, but she has none because no one knows that she is there. When she gets hugs from people, she can hardly feel it because of her metal costume, and when people give her a compliment, she doesn't feel very good about it because the compliment is meant for the robot she is pretending to be, not the real her. Everybody is always talking about what the robot did, and nobody ever talks about Cindy. Cindy feels trapped inside her robot costume, but she is afraid to come out. Maybe all of the friends she made as the robot won't want to be friends with Cindy. Being a robot (or hiding behind a wall of lies) might be lonely, but at least it keeps you safe from things like rejection and bad feelings.

Many victims feel lonely and trapped behind their wall of lies, just like Cindy felt in her robot costume. The walls they put up to keep the bad things from hurting them also keep the good things from helping them. The walls keep out the good things as well as the bad.

Keeping up a wall of lies can also affect your self-esteem in a bad way. For example, if you lie and tell people you got an "A" on your history test when you really got a "D," it doesn't matter how much people compliment you on studying hard or tell you how smart you are; it won't make you feel any better about yourself because you didn't really do the thing you are getting the compliments on. The compliments might even cause you to feel worse about yourself because you might feel bad about lying and ashamed that in real life you got a bad grade on the test. Some victims feel guilty about the lies they have told. A victim who has lied a lot may start to believe that she is a bad person because of her lying. Telling lies doesn't make you a bad person; lies are a way of trying to protect yourself when there is abuse in your life. Trying to protect yourself is good, but lying will just end up hurting you and the people around you. It's important to try to quit lying, especially if you are no longer being abused.

While a person is being abused, lying might sometimes keep her from getting hurt, or it might only seem like it is keeping her from getting hurt. In reality, lying about the abuse may have been actually keeping her from getting help. If you are a victim who has lied to keep the abuse a secret, you may feel tempted to blame yourself for not telling about the abuse sooner or getting help sooner. Not telling about the abuse *does not* mean you asked for the abuse or wanted the abuse to keep happening; it means you were trying to keep yourself safe. Lying is a *defense mechanism* that many abuse victims learn to use in order to survive. If you have become good at lying, you will probably be able to keep the people around you from finding out about the abuse. Don't forget, lying about the abuse might be keeping you from getting help and support because people can't help you if they don't know what is wrong.

To summarize, lying is a way that abuse victims try to keep themselves safe from more hurt. Lying about how you really feel and what is really going on in your life can cause you to feel lonely, isolated, and like no one cares. It can keep you from experiencing real friendship, cause you to feel bad about yourself, and lower your self-esteem. Lying about being abused and keeping the abuse a secret can keep you from getting help and support and makes it easier for the offender to molest others. If you really want to recover from the hurt of the abuse, you must work hard on being honest. It won't work any other way.

Dissociation

Victims of trauma learn many ways of coping with the hurtful things that are happening to them. One coping mechanism that is common to victims of sexual assault is called *dissociation*. Dissociation, or "spacing out," means mentally and emotionally moving away from here-and-now reality. The ability to dissociate is very useful if you are being sexually abused. Dissociating helps the victim get away mentally and emotionally from the hurtful things that are happening, making the abuse easier to deal with for the time being. There is more than one way to dissociate. It is possible to dissociate from physical sensations so you don't feel anything in your body, or to dissociate from emotions so you don't have any feelings, or to dissociate from reality so you aren't fully aware of what's going on around you. Some people experience all three types of dissociation at once. The different types can be experienced one at a time or all at the same time.

People also have different styles of dissociating. Some have an imaginary world that they go into when they dissociate, some have the sensation of leaving their bodies and becoming a part of something in the room such as the walls, or some simply focus on only one thing, blocking out everything else. A person who is dissociated is not feeling the full impact of what is happening to her, and many survivors report it feels as if they are somehow separate from their bodies or that they "go away" when they dissociate. Other survivors report that it feels as if they are in a dream, and what is happening to them isn't real. Some survivors describe feeling like they are outside of the situation watching someone else being abused. Feeling like you aren't a part of your body (being dissociated from your body) can be compared to the relationship between a car and its driver.

As an example, a driver controls the speed and movement of a car, but the driver is not part of the car; she is separate from it. Even though she isn't a part of the car, the driver is concerned about the condition of the car because she depends on the car to get her where she wants to go. What happens to the car while she is in it affects her; if the car goes over a cliff, she goes over with it. If someone were to come along and start hitting the car with a sledgehammer, the driver would feel the vibrations from the car being hit but would not feel the actual blows. The driver would probably be upset that her car was getting hit but not as upset as she would be if she herself were being hit with a sledgehammer. A person dissociated from her body feels kind of like the driver of the car in this example, separate from her body, the body that gets her from one place to another.

If you dissociate or space out, it is important for you to realize that when you do, you don't notice what is going on around you as much as you normally do, so it becomes easier for you to get hurt. If you are busy trying to be in your imaginary world where it is safe, you might forget to be careful in ways that will help keep you safe in the real world, such as looking to see if any cars are coming before you cross the street or watching what's going on around you so you can get help if someone is trying to hurt you. Being dissociated causes you to not notice what is going on around you as much, so you are less able to take care of yourself. This lack of awareness and not being able to take care of yourself is the same thing that causes so many injuries among those who are drunk and/or high; it can be very dangerous. Take care of yourself as best you can.

Emotions

Being sexually abused causes a person to have a lot of very strong feelings. Most victims learn very fast to stuff their feelings. As soon as a feeling comes up, the survivor stuffs it right back down again. Many survivors get so far away from their feelings they don't even know that they have feelings anymore. When they try to think about how they are feeling, all they feel is numb or empty inside.

If you can think of times when it seemed like everyone around you was having feelings except for you, you are probably detached from your feelings. For example, one of your close friends has a healthy baby, and everyone around you feels happy, but you don't feel anything. So you pretend to feel happy so that people around you won't think you're weird.

There are a number of reasons survivors learn not to feel. Most offenders tell their victims to keep the abuse a secret and not to tell anyone. If the victim went around acting upset because she got abused, other people would keep asking her what's wrong, and they might find out about the abuse. So the victim learns to put on an act like everything is OK so that no one will find out. Some offenders get angry and hurt their victims worse if they cry, or get angry or upset. In this case, the victim learns to stuff her feeling to keep from getting hurt worse. Many victims learn not to feel simply because their feelings about the abuse are too hard for them to deal with all alone. As long as the abuse remains a secret, the victim must deal with it alone because part of keeping the secret is not being able to talk to anyone about it, which keeps the victim alone and prevents her from getting help and support from other people.

People who are detached from their feelings still have some feelings; they just don't have them all that often, and they don't have very many different kinds of feelings. For example, a survivor may only let herself have a few different kinds of feelings, such as feeling angry, tired, hungry, and good. She might limit herself to just those feelings because those are the only ones it seems OK to have. She might believe that if she felt all the bad feelings she was having when she was being abused, like feeling scared, ashamed, sad, and hurt, those feelings would be so strong she wouldn't be able to control them. For a survivor of abuse, not being in control is not safe. So the survivor decides not to let herself have these feelings at all because it's just not safe.

Many survivors believe that they don't have any feelings about their abuse. All human be- ings have feelings; some of us allow ourselves to feel all of our feelings, and some of us bury most of our feelings, only allowing ourselves to feel a few "safe" ones now and then. Survivors who believe they have no feelings about their abuse are usually people who have learned how to bury many of their feelings so deep, so fast, that they don't really even know these feelings exist. For example, let's say that a stranger buries some treasure 10 feet under a baseball field. One day, the stranger comes up to you and tells you there is treasure in that baseball field, so you get a bunch of people and you search every inch of that baseball field over and over and find nothing. Because you searched so hard and found nothing, you decide that there must not be any treasure there; the stranger must be wrong. But the truth is that there is treasure there, you just couldn't see it because it was buried too deep, just like some feelings that are buried so deep you think there isn't anything there.

Here is a real-life example of a survivor who has stuffed her feelings very deep. Tasha's abuse started when she was only 4. Tasha learned to stuff her feelings at a very young age because whenever she would start crying because the abuse hurt and made her feel sad, her offender would hit Tasha and call her names until she pretended like everything was fine. Now Tasha is 15, and whenever she thinks about her abuse, she doesn't feel anything but numb and empty inside. Tasha feels weird about not feeling anything. She has seen other girls talk about their abuse and they always cry and look upset. Tasha thinks she should be upset and sad when she remembers her abuse, but she just isn't. Whenever Tasha considers talking about her abuse, she stops herself because she's afraid no one will believe her, or even worse, they might think that she wanted the abuse all because she doesn't have any feelings when she talks about it.

If you are a person who doesn't feel any emotions about the abuse, this may mean that your emotions are still buried, and you simply aren't quite ready to deal with them yet. Stuffing emotions and not feeling anything about the abuse is a defense that some survivors use to try and protect themselves from feeling emotional hurt.

The problem with keeping feelings buried is that it takes energy. It's a natural human tendency to feel our emotions, just like it's a natural human tendency to breathe. If you try to quit breathing and hold your breath, at first it's pretty easy, but as the seconds tick by it takes more and more effort to keep yourself from taking a breath, just like it takes effort for a person to keep feelings buried. Many survivors complain that they always feel tired and don't know why. They generally feel tired because keeping their feelings buried is using up lots of their energy.

A survivor may come to believe that she is a "bad person" because of her lack of feelings. For example, Mary's best friend gets killed in a car accident. She goes to the funeral and everyone is crying and sad, but she can't cry and she doesn't feel anything. Mary starts thinking things like, "I must be a pretty insensitive jerk; I don't even feel sad when my best friend dies. I don't even deserve to have friends." So the survivor puts herself down because she doesn't feel any emotion.

Another problem with stuffing feelings is that good feelings are blocked out along with the bad ones. When you stuff your feelings, it's kind of like you have built a giant wall around your heart with no doors in it so that no bad feelings can get in and hurt you. This wall does its job well; no bad feelings can get in, but the problem is that no good feelings can get in either. There may be people in your life who have given you love and support, but you couldn't feel it because those feelings couldn't get through the wall. So your wall that blocks out feelings such as hurt and shame also blocks out feelings like love, support, acceptance, and pride. Many times when people believe that they are all alone and no one cares, it's because their walls are up and no one from the outside can break through.

For a survivor who is detached from her feelings to get in touch with them again, she must really believe that it is pretty safe for her to do so, and she must be willing to take a risk. Making changes always involves some amount of risk. The following are fears common to those who want to start feeling their emotions again instead of stuffing them.

If I felt my emotions . . .

I would have to face some facts I don't want
    to face.
I wouldn't be able to control them.
I wouldn't be able to stop crying.
I might say or do something I shouldn't.
I might feel angry or resentful toward people I

love.

I might get really depressed.

I would feel like a wimp, baby, stupid idiot, and
so on.

People would be able to hurt me easier.

I would have to feel bad feelings like hurt and
guilt.

People will find out I'm not really tough and
look down on me.

People will think I'm stupid and reject me.

I won't be able to protect myself.

Fears such as these don't just go away on their
own; these fears must be dealt with before the
survivor will let any scary feelings come out.
Talking to someone you trust about your
fears, plus getting their support and reassur-
ance, can help you find the strength and courage needed to take a risk and let your feelings
come out so that you can deal with them
better.

Trust

When an adult sexually abuses a child, that adult violates the child's trust. Adults are supposed to protect children, but when they abuse them instead, the child learns not to trust others. Having trouble trusting people is a normal aftereffect of sexual abuse that can make life more difficult. Feeling like you can't trust people means that it takes longer to make real friends. It's harder to show others the real you; it's harder to be honest about your feelings and what is really going on with you.

Being abused teaches victims not to trust others; some offenders also teach us not to trust ourselves. For example, a little girl named Tanya gets sexually abused by her uncle. Tanya tells her uncle that the sex hurts and she doesn't like it. The uncle tells Tanya that she is wrong, sex feels good, and of course she likes it, he can tell she does just by looking at her. Besides, everyone likes sex, he tells her. Tanya thinks her uncle must know what he's talking about because he's an adult. And she sees on TV and in movies that people are supposed to like sex.

Tanya decides that it probably doesn't really hurt, she's just being a wimp, and she's probably just too stupid to know what feels good and what doesn't. Tanya's offender has taught her not to trust her own thoughts, feelings, and body sensations. So Tanya grows up not trusting herself; she thinks she must depend on others to tell her what she thinks and feels. It robs her of her independence and her sense of who she is. Not being able to trust yourself means you don't always believe your own thoughts and feelings, you put yourself down a lot, and you tend to be too dependent on other people.

If being able to trust is a problem for you, it's important to give yourself time. After someone you trusted has hurt you so bad, it is very hard to learn to trust other people again. After believing for so long that you can't trust your own thoughts and feelings, it takes a long time to learn that you really can trust them.

Learning to trust yourself again is a process that's too long and complicated to fully explain here, but the first step in the process is awareness. This awareness is knowing that you have a tendency not to trust your own thoughts and feelings. The next step is learning to catch yourself in the act of denying your own true thoughts and feelings. Once you can catch yourself doing this, you can make choices to start trusting yourself.

Learning to trust other people again is also a long and difficult process. The first step is learning some standards for figuring out who can generally be trusted and who can't. Of course, you can never be 100% sure if someone is trustworthy or not, but there are ways to stack the odds in your favor. The following questions can help you decide if you should trust a person or not:

— Does this person use people? Does he treat people like dirt or cut them down?
— When you say no to this person, does he respect that or does he try to pressure you into doing things you don't want to?
— Is this person honest or does she lie to people?
— Does this person have a history of abusing others emotionally, physically, or sexually? Is this person ever violent?
— Does this person break the law?
— Does this person show respect for your feelings and beliefs?
— Does this person give you support or tear you down?
— Is this person clean and sober?
— Do you ever feel the need to lie or make excuses for this person? Does she ask you to lie to others?
— Does this person want you to keep secrets? Is there any part of your relationship with him that is secret?
— Does this person ever encourage or enable you to do things that are against the law or unsafe?

[78]

Once you decide who you are pretty sure you can trust, the next step is to take the risk and trust them with something small. You don't have to trust the person with everything at once. Start with something little and if they pass this test, try something a little harder and go from there. Learning to trust is a process that goes one step at a time; if you take it slowly, you should find success.

Self-Image

Self-image is what you feel about yourself, what you think about yourself, and what you believe to be true about yourself. For example, do you think of yourself as a good person or a bad person? Do you like yourself or hate yourself? Do you think you are smart or not too bright? This is the kind of information that makes up your self-image. Being sexually abused can affect your self-image in both sexual ways and nonsexual ways.

A pretty big part of a person's self-image tends to come from how other people treat us and react to us. Offenders do not treat their victims with respect, so because we are not treated with respect, we might start believing that we aren't worthy of respect or that we don't deserve any better. So when people treat us like dirt, we tend not to say or do anything about it because we don't believe we deserve any better. On the other hand, if we meet someone who treats us with respect, we may do something to break off the relationship, perhaps because we believe it can't last because it seems too good to be true or maybe it feels uncomfortable because we are so used to being treated badly.

An offender tends to treat his victims like objects. He uses a person's body to satisfy his desires without even thinking about the fact that he is hurting someone. He doesn't consider what she wants or doesn't want. He doesn't think about how it makes her feel when he forces sex on her. The victim is treated like a "thing" that has no feelings to hurt, no nerves to feel pain, no spirit to feel broken, no soul to feel ashamed. This is exactly how a person might treat an object. No one considers what an object thinks or how it feels because objects don't think or feel. When a person is treated like an object, such as being sexually abused, that person learns to believe that her thoughts, feelings, wants, and needs don't count. A person who has learned these beliefs tends to do things she doesn't think are right, treats herself badly, and often has little or no respect for herself.

When an abuse victim is treated like an object by her offender, it can completely change the way she feels about herself (self-image). Many victims come out of the abuse feeling like they are bad and worthless, like in this next example. Summer always thought of herself as a pretty good kid who was happy most of the time. All of this changed after Summer got molested.

When Summer's offender molested her, she thought the sex was a punishment for doing something really bad, even though she couldn't think of anything she had done wrong. Over time, the abuse kept happening and Summer thought less and less of herself as a person. Her offender didn't seem to care that it made her body hurt when he had sex with her, or that forcing sex on her made her feel ashamed and dirty. Summer figured she must be a bad person if she wasn't worth caring about. Sometimes the offender would get mad at her for not taking her clothes off fast enough, and then Summer would feel mad at herself for not even being able to take her clothes off right. Once Summer's clothes were off she felt cold, but when she told her offender she was cold, he would say, "Quit being such a wimp, it's not cold." Summer would say to herself, "Why am I such a big sissy, why can't I be tough like a normal person and just handle it? I shouldn't be cold."

The offender kept on telling Summer that the things she thought and felt and did were wrong, when actually her thoughts, feelings, and actions were perfectly normal for what she was going through. Because of the feelings the abuse created in her and the way the offender treated her, Summer felt like a person who was worthless and bad. Summer went from a kid who was happy and thought she was good, to a kid who hated herself and just wanted to crawl into a hole and die. The abuse completely changed her feelings about herself and how she deserved to be treated by others.

Sexual abuse can also affect the way people see themselves in relation to their sexuality. Many offenders give their victims the message, directly or indirectly, that all the victim is good for is sex. He may get her to believe that the only way she can get friends, affection, and attention is to allow people to use her sexually. For example, on the outside, Angie looks like a happy person who likes to have fun, but on the inside Angie tells herself she must be one of the stupidest, ugliest people on the face of the earth. She hated herself and couldn't imagine why anybody would want to have anything to do with her. She thought she had nothing to offer that anyone would want, except maybe sex. Angie's offender had told her that she was great in bed, which was a good thing, according to him, because she couldn't do anything else right, in his opinion. Angie believed that the only way she could get people to really like her was to give them sex, so that's what she gave them.

Angie always wore as little as possible to get the guys' attention. She would talk dirty to them and tell them that she would have sex with them any way they wanted in hopes that they would keep liking her and giving her attention. Most of the time, Angie didn't even try to make friends with girls because, since girls didn't want sex from her, she just knew there was nothing about her they would like, so almost all of her friends were guys. Angie enjoyed the attention she got when she hung out with the guys, flirting with them and sometimes having sex. When the evening was over and Angie was left by herself, she always felt bad about what she had done and called herself a whore. It's not that Angie feels good about sleeping around with so many different guys; she hates herself for it, but she doesn't seem to be able to stop even though she wants to. The reason Angie can't seem to stop sleeping around is because her offender taught her to believe that sex is the only thing that makes her a worthwhile person. Angie knows in her head that she can get friendship, love, and attention without giving people sex; it's just that her heart doesn't quite believe it yet. Being sexually abused has taught Angie to only value herself for her sexuality.

Being sexually abused can affect your attitude toward your body. Many victims learn to make their bodies feel numb to separate themselves from their bodies. A victim who tries to keep her body numb and doesn't have much respect for herself may let people beat her and physically abuse her body, or she may even hurt her own body by cutting on herself or doing other things. She may act like she doesn't care about her body, not even bothering to protect it or take care of it. Some victims feel like their bodies are dirty and bad because of the awful things their bodies have been forced to do during the abuse. Because of this, the victim may hate her body and have no respect for it so she doesn't treat it very well.

To be healthy, it's important to treat your body and yourself with respect and to make sure that others do the same. Although your self-image is affected by the way you are treated by others, the way other people treat you is also affected by how you feel about yourself. A person who has no respect for herself is much more likely to be taken advantage of than a person who is confident and willing to stand up for herself. A good first step to improve your self-image is to start treating yourself better and showing yourself some respect.

Relationships and Sexuality

Being sexually abused can affect your relationships and sexuality in a lot of ways. This section tells about the ways abuse affects some of those relationships. It gives examples of the types of sexual relationships survivors tend to get into before they get help. It also covers how some survivors learn to use sex to get their needs met, needs such as self-esteem, attention, and power and control.

There are lots of reasons why former victims will often get into relationships and stay in relationships where they are abused and treated like dirt. A common pattern for former victims of abuse is explained in the following example. Amy was a part of a group of kids from her school who hung out together. Amy was a nice person and she liked to make people happy. Amy had a self-esteem problem; she didn't like herself very much. Because Amy felt bad about herself, she believed she wouldn't have any friends at all unless she did everything she could to make her friends happy. One way Amy knew to make people happy was to have sex with them. Amy slept with some of, well, actually, most of the guys in her group of friends from time to time because that always seemed to make them happy and make them like her. Anytime Amy felt lonely and wanted attention all she had to do was tell one of her friends she would have sex with him and BINGO, instant attention!

Amy loved her friends, but none of them ever seemed to mind that she slept with so many guys just as long as they got their share. Most of the time, Amy felt good when she was being sexual with a guy, but afterward she would feel lonely, dirty, and empty inside.

Sometimes Amy didn't even feel like having sex at all, but she would do it even though she hated it because she was afraid her friends wouldn't like her as much if she didn't.

Whenever Amy met new guys, she would always say to herself, "No matter what, I'm not having sex with this guy. We will be like normal friends are supposed to be, hang out together but not have sex." Despite Amy's promise to herself, it never seemed to turn out that way; somehow she would always end up having sex with the guy.

Because she couldn't seem to say no to sex once she had decided she liked a guy, Amy concluded that it must mean she is a hopeless slut. Amy felt bad about herself because she has sex with too many guys. After a while, Amy doesn't even try to say no; what's the use, she decides, she's slept with so many guys it doesn't even matter anymore. Amy no longer has any respect for herself.

There are many reasons why victims of abuse tend to act out in sexual ways like in the example above. Being sexually abused teaches its victims to never say no to sex and to use sex to get certain needs met that should be met in other ways. This next example shows why it is sometimes difficult for abuse survivors to say no to sex.

The first time her uncle tried to have sex with Dana she told him no, but it didn't do any good, he had sex with her anyway. Dana kept saying no every time her uncle would do stuff to her, but he never listened. Then one day when Dana told her uncle no, he said, "You have no right to tell me no," and he hit her really hard.

From these experiences with her uncle, Dana comes to believe that saying no to sex doesn't do any good because people will have sex with her anyway, no matter what she says. Dana learned from her uncle that saying no to sex might even get her hit. So whenever a guy starts trying to get Dana to have sex, she doesn't say no because she is afraid of getting beat up. Saying no to sex has never done her any good. Dana figures other guys will just have sex with her anyway, just like her uncle always did.

Because of her abuse, Dana has trouble saying no to sex, and she ends up being sexual with lots of guys when she really doesn't want to. Word spreads that it's easy to get sex with Dana so she ends up with a reputation as a skank and getting used and abused by even more people. Dana feels really awful about herself. This problem of Dana's continued until she got some help with healing from her abuse.

When a person is forced to have sex against her will, especially at a young age, when she is not yet physically or emotionally ready to do so, sex becomes a very confusing thing. Sexual abuse can affect a person's sexuality in lots of different ways. *Sexuality* is what a person does, thinks, believes, and feels in regard to sex. There is a big difference between healthy sexuality and unhealthy sexuality. Unfortunately, most survivors have been taught just about everything there is to know about unhealthy sexuality from their offenders and don't really learn what healthy sexuality is. Because we learned the wrong things about sexuality from being abused, we may use sex in ways that are bad for us or bad for other people. We may use sex for things it wasn't meant to be used for, so it doesn't meet our needs very well. There are many basic human needs that survivors try to take care of by using sex.

All human beings have a need to feel good about themselves and to get compliments for things they do well. We all want to be loved and feel wanted. We all need attention and affection. Many survivors believe that the only way they can get these needs met is through sex.

For example, Tracy was sexually abused by a guy named Dan. Whenever Dan made Tracy have sex, he always told her how pretty she was, how much he needed her, and how great she was in bed. Tracy hated it when Dan made her have sex, but the compliments and attention she got felt good sometimes. Tracy learned from her abuse that sex was a quick way to get attention, affection, and compliments. So whenever Tracy was having one of those days where she felt ugly and fat and worthless, she would go out and get a guy to have sex with her so that he would give her some attention and hugs and say nice things to her. Tracy knew that guys would just say the nice things and pay attention to her so that they could get sex, but it still made her feel better for a little while. She figured the only way she was going to get anyone to give her affection and tell her nice things about herself was to offer sex in exchange.

Many survivors feel like Tracy. Because of being abused, they may come to believe that the only reason anyone would want them is for sex, so they trade sex for affection and compliments. Or they might believe that sex is the only thing they can do really well, so they trade sex for attention and the feeling of being worth something. The following is a list, which is related to self-esteem, of other reasons survivors use sex:

— To feel wanted or needed
— To feel like I'm good for something
— To feel loved
— To get affection
— To show off that I'm good in bed
— To prove I can get a guy/girl if I want one
— To feel older
— So people will like me/to get friends
— To prove to myself I am sexually attractive
— To get compliments and attention
— To prove the abuse didn't affect me

To help protect themselves while they were being abused, many survivors learned to dissociate. To dissociate means to space out or to make your mind go somewhere else. Some people can even make their bodies go numb when they dissociate. Many survivors automatically dissociate anytime someone gets sexual with them. Survivors who have this automatic reaction may seek out sex because it makes them dissociate. For them, dissociation is a way to become comfortably numb, a way of escaping what is going on in the real world when things get depressing.

Some survivors don't go as far as dissociating, but they do use sex as a distraction. They use sex to get their minds off something or as a way of avoiding bad thoughts or feelings. For example, Toni starts thinking about how pissed off her mom is going to be when she finds out that Toni got suspended from school again. Toni doesn't want to think about that so she goes and has sex with someone to get her mind off it.

Some survivors try really hard to convince themselves that sex is no big deal. Believing that sex is no big deal makes being sexually abused seem not so bad, so this belief is a way of trying to cope with sexual abuse. A survivor who uses this way of coping will often use sex simply as a form of entertainment or a way to pass the time when she feels bored. She may keep having sex a lot to prove to herself that sex is no big deal and, therefore, prove the abuse wasn't a big deal either.

From our offenders, we learn that sex can be used very effectively as a means of power and control. Offenders use sex as a weapon; a way to hurt and degrade and show anger. We learn that sex can hurt us and that sex can be used to hurt someone else. The following is a list of ways survivors sometimes use sex for power, control, and the expression of anger:

— To hurt, punish, or degrade myself or someone else
— To get revenge or make someone mad or jealous
— To make a relationship more binding/make someone mine
— To make someone notice me/get attention
— As a power trip/to feel powerful

— As a form of rebellion
— To distract someone/get them off track

To a survivor who believes that all she is good for is sex, her body is like a thing that can be bought, sold, or traded. She may use her body to get something she wants or needs, such as food or clothes. She may feel that she does not deserve kindness and uses her body to "pay back" people who have been nice to her.

In this last section, we have learned about several unhealthy ways survivors use sex. This section has also explained about how survivors sometimes have trouble saying no to sex and types of relationships survivors commonly get into. If you are a survivor and you find yourself using sex in unhealthy ways, it is important to learn new ways of getting your needs met, ways that are safer and leave you feeling happy instead of bad. As you begin to heal from the negative effects of the abuse, you will learn that you deserve love, respect, and kindness and that you don't have to use your body to get these things or to deserve them.

Because people are all different, people react differently to being abused. Some people become more sexual, like in the examples above, and others decide they don't want anything to do with sex at all. Both types of reactions are normal for people who have been abused. The following is an example of a survivor who reacts to her feelings about the abuse by staying away from relationships that could involve anything sexual.

Cindy was molested by her sister's boyfriend when she was 15 years old. Before her abuse, Cindy dated a lot and enjoyed having boyfriends. After being sexually abused, Cindy decided she didn't want anything to do with dating or boyfriends anymore. For Cindy, dating led to boyfriends, and boyfriends led to things like slow dancing and kissing and sometimes even having sex. Ever since the abuse, even the thought of being physically close to a guy turned her stomach.

Most of Cindy's friends had boyfriends, and this made Cindy feel kind of weird and left out, especially when her friends went to dances or went together on double dates. She felt like she wasn't really part of the group anymore. Cindy still had male friends, but anytime a guy showed interest in being more than friends, she would act cold toward him and keep her distance.

If you are a survivor who has reacted to your abuse kind of like Cindy, it's important to know that your reaction is a normal one. This type of reaction is a way of trying to keep yourself safe after the abuse, and trying to stay safe is good. Many survivors who have this reaction end up deciding that they want to have romantic relationships again, after some time has gone by and they have done some healing and recovering.

Sexuality can be a confusing thing for teens, and being sexually abused can make it even more confusing. One thing that can make sexuality particularly confusing is if a heterosexual person is molested by someone of the same gender, such as a girl being molested by another girl. For example, Andrea was in the fourth grade when she and her family moved to a new neighborhood. Andrea was anxious to make new friends, but the only other kid in the neighborhood was a girl named Crystal who was 3 years older than Andrea. Even though their ages were 3 years apart, the two girls started to hang out together.

After the girls had been friends for a couple of months, Crystal told Andrea they were going to play a new "game." Crystal told Andrea that in this game, she had to do whatever Crystal told her to do or she would get beat up. Crystal also said that if Andrea didn't keep the game a secret, Crystal would make up a whole bunch of bad things about Andrea and tell them to Andrea's parents and all the kids at school.

While playing this game, Crystal would order Andrea to take her clothes off and then she would do sexual things to her. At first Andrea was so afraid and confused about what was happening, she didn't even try to resist Crystal. Later on, Andrea tried to say no to Crystal, but every time she did, Crystal would push her and hit her and make more threats.

Crystal continued to abuse Andrea sexually until Andrea's family moved after about 3 years. Andrea was happy when her family moved; now that she was away from Crystal and the abuse, she thought her problems were over. However, Andrea was disappointed to find that even though the abuse wasn't happening anymore, it still bothered her. Andrea had seen TV shows about sexual abuse, so she knew it happened to lots of girls, but it seemed the offenders were always men or boys. Andrea had never heard of a girl being molested by another girl before. Did this mean she was a lesbian? Had she done something to make Crystal feel attracted to her? Was it all her fault? Andrea wondered about all of these things. She felt confused and alone and didn't know what to do.

Although it's true that most sex offenders are male, sometimes females also molest people. If you are a person who has been molested by someone of your own gender, you are not the only one this has happened to. You deserve help like all abuse survivors do. Being sexually abused by a person of your own gen- der does not make you a homosexual (gay), just like being abused by a person of the opposite sex doesn't make you heterosexual (straight). No matter what kind of person your offender is, sexual abuse can cause lots of feelings and confusion about sexuality. Talking to a counselor or adult you trust about these thoughts and feelings can help you sort things out and feel less confused.

School Problems

Being abused will often cause victims to have some problems in school. Many times victims blame themselves for their school problems because they don't know that being abused often causes people to have trouble in school. There are lots of ways abuse can cause problems for people in school.

The school problems may be the result of an effect of the abuse called *post-traumatic stress disorder* or PTSD for short. PTSD is a group of symptoms that people sometimes get when they have had something really bad happen to them such as abuse. Triggers, panic attacks, flashbacks, bad dreams, and intrusive thoughts and memories are all things that can happen to people who have PTSD. These symptoms of PTSD can cause problems for people in school.

One symptom of PTSD that can cause problems is intrusive thoughts or memories. Intrusive thoughts or memories means that thoughts about the abuse or memories of abuse will all of a sudden pop into your head and you can't seem to get them out of your head no matter how hard you try.

When these bad memories or thoughts of abuse invade the victim's head, it becomes almost impossible to think about anything else. For an abuse victim, this means that if you happen to be in school when one of these abuse thoughts or memories hits you, you won't be able to concentrate on your school work, and you will miss out on whatever the class is doing at the time. Missing out on what the class is doing might cause problems like getting in trouble for not paying attention, feeling frustrated or stupid, bad grades, or not getting your work done as fast. Feeling really upset and afraid because of the abuse (panic attack), or seeing the abuse in your head and feeling like you are back in the abuse (flashback), also makes it close to impossible to concentrate in class.

For example, Sue is doing a worksheet in English class. She goes up to her teacher's desk to ask him a question when she discovers that the teacher is wearing the same kind of cologne that her offender always wore. The smell of this cologne triggers Sue and suddenly she feels scared and shaky. Sue takes her assignment back to her desk, but she just can't concentrate on her work. In her head she remembers all of the stuff Jon, her offender, did to her the last time he molested her. She tries as hard as she can to concentrate on her school work but she just can't think straight.

Sue just wants all of the bad stuff in her head to go away so she can do her work like the other kids. Sue thinks to herself, "I've tried everything I know to make the memories go away, but nothing ever works. It's like I can't even get away from him at school." Sue looks around the class and sees that all of her friends are just about done with the worksheet. Sue looks at her own paper, where she is still on the third question. Sue says to herself, "I hate this. I'm so stupid, I never finish in time."

Sue's teacher starts walking around the room, collecting the assigned worksheets. Sue sees the teacher coming her way, so she starts circling answers as fast as she can. The teacher sees Sue just circling any old answer and decides to confront her on it. Frowning, the teacher says, "You didn't finish your work again and now you're just circling answers without even reading the questions. I'm really disappointed in you." Sue feels ashamed and stressed out. Not knowing what else to do, she makes up an excuse for her unfinished work. Sue tells the teacher she didn't finish her work because she had a really bad headache, but she didn't want to get in trouble for not finishing her work so she just started circling answers. In trying to deal with the symptoms of her PTSD, Sue ends up not finishing her work, lying to her teacher, and feeling like she's stupid.

Like Sue, many survivors have times they can't pay attention in class because thoughts or memories of their abuse are just too strong.

The following is a list of problems that survivors often have in school because of PTSD:

— Not being able to concentrate
— Not getting work done on time
— Feeling frustrated or stupid
— Bad grades
— Trouble understanding the work
— Being told you are lazy or slow

Some of the negative ways that victims sometimes try to cope with these school problems include

— Lying/making up excuses
— Skipping school
— Getting mad at the teacher
— Quitting school
— Acting like you don't care
— Refusing to do school work
— Answering questions in a smart-aleck way because you don't know the real answer
— Blaming other people or situations for not getting your work done or not paying attention

There are other effects of sexual abuse that can cause problems in school too, things like feeling scared, feeling bad about yourself, or just not being able to think straight. For example, Patty knows there is a restraining order against Jack, the man who molested her, but it doesn't make her feel any safer. Patty is always afraid that Jack is going to get her because she told about the abuse.

In her first-period class, the teacher is reviewing the stuff that will be on the next test, but Patty can't seem to stay with the teacher's review for more than a couple of minutes at a time. She keeps finding herself watching the door to the classroom and the window to the outside for any signs of Jack. After a while Patty tells herself, "I can't keep looking for Jack; I have to concentrate on this review. I'm going to quit looking at the door and window and I'm going to make myself keep my eyes straight ahead looking at the teacher."

It was hard, but Patty was able to keep herself looking straight ahead. Even though she was looking straight at the teacher, she found herself picturing the layout of the classroom in her mind and trying to plan how she would escape if Jack came through the door and what she would do if she saw him in the window.

She still couldn't get herself to focus on the review.

In her next class, Patty was able to focus a bit better on school. She felt safer in this room because it had no windows and it was close to the office. Patty liked this class and knew the subject well. However, every time she would start to raise her hand to answer a question, she would think about Jack always telling her she was stupid and saying she didn't know anything, and she would keep the hand she was about to raise glued to the desk. Patty would think, "Jack's right, if I got called on I'd probably say something stupid, I probably just think I know the answer. I hate myself and everybody else probably hates me too. If they don't they are stupid."

As you can see from the above example, Patty's poor self-esteem and her fear of Jack keep her from concentrating and participating in her classes most of the time. These are things that affect her grades and her ability to learn in school. If you think abuse is causing you some problems in school like the people in the example, it might help to tell a teacher or school counselor whom you trust about it.

[111]

You can ask them to read this section of the book and show them the appendix on page 131 to help them understand so they can help you.

Recovery

Lots of people who have been sexually abused never get any help in dealing with what happened to them. They don't get any help, so the effects of the abuse don't go away. There are many reasons why some victims never get help.

Some victims never get help because they never tell anyone about the abuse. They keep the abuse a secret even though it still causes them to have bad feelings inside. Most survivors don't get help until they tell someone about the abuse or the abuse is discovered in some other way. This is because it's hard for a person to give you help and support about the abuse if he or she doesn't even know you were abused. If you want help with the abuse, the first step is to tell an adult you trust about what happened.

Sexual abuse is an awful thing to have happen to you. Most survivors don't like to be reminded that it happened let alone have to think about it or talk about it. It is very normal to feel like you don't even want to think about abuse. This feeling of not wanting to face what happened is another reason why some people don't get help.

Other survivors believe that there is nothing that will help make the bad feelings and problems from the abuse go away. They think, "It happened a long time ago; there is nothing anyone can do about it now so why bother." This is a common belief, but the fact is there are things that can be done to make the problems go away and the bad feelings not so bad. It's called recovery.

Recovery is a process; that means that it doesn't happen right away, it happens over time and it takes some work. When a person is sexually abused, it hurts them emotionally deep inside. That hurt continues to cause pain until it gets a chance to heal. Getting counseling and dealing with the abuse is what helps the emotional hurts to heal, and once they are healed, a lot of that hurt goes away.

It's kind of like if you were to get a very bad cut on your arm. Bad cuts hurt, and sometimes you have to go to the doctor and get stitches so that the cut can heal, just like survivors sometimes have to go to a counselor to help their emotional wounds heal. Without stitches, a bad cut might never heal right; it might keep hurting and could even get worse. Without help and counseling, some emotional wounds can't heal either; they just keep hurting and maybe even get worse.

Getting counseling will help your emotional wounds to heal so that you can feel better. You can ask a trusted adult such as a parent, school counselor, pastor, or case worker to help you find a counselor who knows about helping people who have been sexually abused.

In counseling you will probably talk or write or draw about what happened to you, how it made you feel, and some of the problems it has caused for you. If you feel like there is no way you could ever talk about what happened, don't let that keep you from getting help. The counselor will help you talk about it, and you don't have to talk about what happened right away. Most counselors understand how hard it is to talk about abuse at first, and they try their best to make it so that you don't feel too uncomfortable.

Sometimes when people first go into counseling and start talking about the abuse, they find that they feel worse instead of better for a while. This is called *flooding,* and it is a pretty normal thing that happens to some survivors when they first start counseling. Survivors also might find that they start remembering more of the abuse, and they think about it more than they used to.

For example, Jenny finally gets up the courage to tell her mom about the abuse. Jenny's mom is supportive and wants to get help for Jenny so she finds Jenny a counselor. When Jenny first went to counseling, it felt good to not have to keep the whole thing a secret anymore, and she liked knowing that people believed her. It was still hard for Jenny to talk about her abuse, and since she started the counseling it just seemed like she couldn't stop thinking about it. Jenny felt kind of sad and confused. She thought about quitting counseling, but she decided not to because everyone said it would help if she stayed with it. Jenny kept going to counseling and trying to work on the abuse memories with her counselor. Jenny always felt bad when she remembered her abuse, but after a while she noticed that she didn't feel as sad or afraid anymore. Jenny could see she wasn't as grumpy, and she didn't get mad at people as easily. She began doing better in school, her nightmares went away, and talking about the abuse kept getting easier. Jenny was even able to tell some of her friends about her abuse and found out some of them had been through the same thing. Jenny was glad she stayed in counseling because she felt like a much happier person now and the abuse didn't bother her so much anymore.

Like Jenny learned, recovery is all about working to make yourself feel better, and maybe even making some of your problems go away. When a person has been sexually abused, sometimes it feels like there is no way you could ever feel normal again, but believe it or not, it is possible. Recovery will help you get things back to normal so that you can feel happier with yourself and your life. Lots of kids have been sexually abused, and lots of those kids get some help and grow up to have normal, happy lives. With some work, determination, and the right kind of help, you can get back many of the things the abuse has taken away and have one of those normal, happy lives.

Glossary . . .
in Plain English

Many words in the English language have more than one meaning. The words in this glossary are defined in the context they are used in this book only. For additional definitions, use a regular dictionary.

Access   To enter, to get in.

Actual   Real.

Adrenaline,   (Also known as epinephrine.) A
or adrenalin   chemical that is in your body when

something scary or dangerous happens. When adrenaline is in your body, it makes your muscles feel all pumped up and tense, and you feel full of energy. Some people feel a "rush" when their body puts out adrenaline. Adrenaline is kind of like speed; it can pump you up and make you feel like running or fighting, or it can make you jumpy and nervous.

Appealing	Something you like or want.
Assaulted	When someone hurts you on purpose.
Awareness	Knowing what is going on around you.
Broken-record principle	A principle stating that if a person hears the same thing said about herself over and over again, she tends to start believing what she's been hearing even if it's not true.
Common	Something that happens a lot, something normal.
Concentrate	To think hard about something.

Confident   To feel good about yourself.

Coping   Taking care of yourself in a positive way.

Damaged-goods   Feeling bad about your body because
syndrome   of the things that were done to it or
                       said about it during the abuse.

Defense   Strategies that people use to protect
mechanism   themselves from getting hurt emo-
                       tionally. An example of a defense
                       mechanism is if a person convinces
                       herself that being sexually abused
                       was her own fault instead of the
                       offender's. This belief is a defense
                       mechanism because it protects the
                       person from feeling helpless and
                       feeling like she can't trust people
                       not to hurt her.

Defenses   Ways we protect ourselves.

Degrade   To tear someone down in a hurtful way.

Denying   Saying something isn't real when it is.

Dependent   To need someone or something.

Depressant   A type of drug that slows your body
                  down. Alcohol is a depressant.

Detached   Away from.

Dissociation "Spacing out." It's like your body is
                  still in the room but your mind is
                  somewhere else. Some people disso-
                  ciate while they are being abused or
                  while they are in flashbacks.

Distraction   Doing something to get your mind
                  off something else.

Effort   Putting energy into doing something.
                  To try.

Emotions   Feelings.

Enable   To let someone do something.

Encouraging   Trying to get someone to do some-
                  thing.

Endorphin   A natural chemical in your body that
                  makes you feel good.

Female   A girl or woman.

Flashback   Having pictures in your head of your
                    abuse and feeling like it is happening
                    again. A person having a flashback
                    can see the abuse and/or offender;
                    she might hear the sounds, feel the
                    emotions, smell the smells, and even
                    feel the abuse happening again in her
                    body. Flashbacks are scary. See page
                    15 for an example.

Flooding   When lots of abuse memories and
                    feelings start coming up all at once
                    after a person has just started to talk
                    about her abuse or started counsel-
                    ing for her abuse.

Frighten   To scare.

Gender   Male or female.

Guilt   Feeling bad about something you did.

Heterosexual   A person who prefers to have sex
                    with a person of the other gender,
                    such as a man who likes to have sex
                    with a woman or a woman who
                    prefers to have sex with a man.

Homosexual A person who prefers to have sex with a person of the same gender, such as a woman who prefers to have sex with another woman or a man who prefers to have sex with another man.

Hyperventilate To breathe so fast that it feels like you can't get any air.

Hypervigilant Always watching what is going on around you; always keeping an eye out for trouble (kind of like the saying, "sleeping with one eye open").

Imaginary Not real, pretend.

Imitation Fake.

Impossible Something you can't do no matter how hard you try.

Independence Being able to take care of yourself.

Intrusive memories When a memory of your abuse pops into your head from out of nowhere. Intrusive memories tend to stay in your head even though you don't want them to. They tend to be very hard to get rid of.

Invade	To go in forcefully.
Isolated	Away from other people.
Kindness	Being nice.
Male	A boy or man.
Manipulate	Trying to trick or control other people so that they do what you want them to.
Memory gaps	Blank spots in a person's memory.
Method	A way of doing something.
Molested	Sexually abused.
Narcotic	A type of drug that kills pain. Heroin is a narcotic.
Nervousness	Feeling kind of scared and jumpy.
Nonsexual	Has nothing to do with sex.

Numb   Not feeling anything.

Offender   Person who abuses other people.

Panic attack   Your body's reaction to being reminded of your abuse. See pages 9 to 10 for a list of the signs of a panic attack.

Physical   Having to do with your body.

Post-traumatic stress disorder, or PTSD   A name for some of the ways abuse affects people. A person who has PTSD is affected by some of these things:

— Triggers
— Trying not to think about your abuse
— Panic attacks
— Memory gaps
— Flashbacks
— Trouble sleeping
— Intrusive memories
— Depression
— Bad dreams
— Being grumpy

[126]

— Going off when you're mad
— Trouble concentrating
— Feeling jumpy or paranoid

Preservation   Keeping something the way it is now; taking care of it.

Prevent   To keep something from happening.

Recovery   The process of getting help and helping yourself to work on healing emotional wounds that you may have suffered when something hurtful happened in your life. Recovering from sexual abuse makes a person feel better about herself and happier about life.

Savior   A person or thing that saves your life.

Seduction   Trying to get someone to have sex with you.

Self-esteem   How you feel about yourself.

Sensations   Body feelings.

Severe   Bad.

Sexuality   What a person does, thinks, believes, and feels about sex.

Stability   Being normal, keeping it together, and not freaking out.

Status   Being respected by other people because of who you are or what you have.

Stimulant   A type of drug that speeds you up. Cocaine is a stimulant.

Stressful   Hard to deal with.

Temporarily   For a little while.

Threat   Something or someone that might damage or hurt someone else.

Tranquilizer   A type of drug that calms you down. Valium is a tranquilizer.

Trauma   When something really bad happens to someone.

Trembling   When your body shakes.

Trigger	Anything that reminds you of your abuse. Usually, if someone is triggered, she has a panic attack, a flashback, or an intrusive memory. See pages 5 to 7 for examples.
Unknowingly	Without knowing about it.
Vibrations	Shaking.
Victim	Person who was abused.
Violate	To break.
Withholding	Hanging on to something and not letting other people have it.
Wound	A cut.

APPENDIX

Effects of Post-Traumatic Stress Disorder
on Learning in the Classroom

Event	Description	Examples
Trigger	Something or someone in her environment reminds the student of some aspect of her abuse.	Sue approaches her teacher to ask him a question on an assignment and discovers the teacher is wearing the same cologne her offender always wore.
Intrusive memory and/or	A memory of a past abuse incident becomes intrusive, popping into the student's head and remaining despite efforts to get rid of it.	Amy is writing the day and date on her paper and realizes her parents are going out tonight and she will be left with her baby-sitter, Jon, who abuses her. Amy remembers all of the stuff Jon did to her the last time they were left alone together. She tries to get the memory out of her head, but with no success. Amy becomes increasingly upset
		Suddenly, Sue feels extremely frightened, her heart races, and she starts sweating. She doesn't know why she feels so scared and she can't seem to think straight. All she

(continued)

Event	Description	Examples
Panic attack	An overwhelming sense of fear and panic accompanied by the physiological effects of severe anxiety overtakes the student.	knows is she feels like crying and running away because it feels like someone will hurt her if she doesn't get away. as she continues to remember the abuse and think about what he will probably do to her tonight.
Inability to concentrate on the task at hand	The student is overwhelmed by the memory/panic attack and is unable to attend to a class lecture of assigned school work.	Sue returns to her desk with her assignment but finds she is unable to concentrate as the panic attack is much too overpowering. Amy is virtually oblivious to her teacher's lecture. She remains focused on the memory of her abuse and the thoughts and feelings that accompany it.
Learning ceases	Due to the intensity of the abuse memory or panic attack, the student misses information provided in the lecture	Amy misses her teacher's instructions on how to reduce fractions as well as the sample problems done on the board. Sue makes no progress on her assignment to circle all of the nouns in the story. The story is two pages long and she has

		only made it through three sentences.
or is unable to make progress on class work. Attempts to focus on academic tasks are unsuccessful.		
Failure to focus on task at hand creates negative emotions	Amy tries as hard as she can to to listen to what her teacher is lecturing about, but memories of Jon's hands feeling between her legs won't subside. Amy thinks to herself, "I've tried everything I can think of to make the memories go away but nothing ever works. It's like I can't even get away from him at school."	She just wants all of the bad stuff in her head to go away so she can do her work like a normal kid. She tries to concentrate on her worksheet but it doesn't work. It's like all of the stuff in her head is all jumbled up. She just can't stop feeling afraid and confused. All she knows for sure is that she just wants to run away and hide.
Feelings of frustration, anger, and powerlessness are common at this stage due to the student's inability to focus on her school work despite her desire and efforts to do so.		

(continued)

Event	Description	Examples
Self-concept suffers	The student becomes used to seeing her peers finish their work or absorb lecture material, whereas she was unable to. Thus the student labels herself as stupid, inferior, a slow learner, and so on, convincing herself she is incapable of meeting average academic expectations.	All around the classroom Amy sees her friends raising their hands to answer questions and jumping up to do math problems on the board. Amy stares at the board, trying to concentrate, but Jon and all of the bad stuff won't leave her head. Amy thinks to herself, "I hate this! I'm so stupid, I can't understand anything."	Sue looks around and sees that her friend Julie is almost done with her worksheet, and two other friends have finished and have started on the next assignment. She looks at her own paper, where she is still on the third sentence. Sue thinks to herself, "I'm such a retard, I can never finish fast enough."
Short-term consequences	The student experiences the short-term consequences of missing the lecture	Amy's teacher asks her a question about the lecture material and Amy is unable to	Sue's teacher begins walking around the room and collecting the worksheets. Sue

	information or not getting the classwork done. Common consequences include being laughed at for not being able to answer simple questions on lecture material, getting bad grades for the day's lesson, and being labeled by others as lazy, slow, or unmotivated.	answer it correctly. Amy feels embarrassed and stupid for not being able to answer such a simple question. Amy thinks the other kids are probably whispering to each other about what an idiot she is.	sees the teacher approaching and begins to circle answers randomly as fast as she can. The teacher spots Sue quickly circling answers and goes to confront her. Frowning, the teacher says, "Once again you didn't finish your work and now you're just circling any old answer. I'm really disappointed in you."
Student attempts to cover up not paying attention and associated emotions	The student attempts to cover up her problem and the feelings that accompany it. Common methods students use in trying to cover up the elements of PTSD are as follows:	Amy becomes defensive. Masking her feelings of inferiority with anger, she lashes out at the teacher, hoping to make her inattentiveness seem intentional to save face in front of her peers. Amy says	Sue feels ashamed of herself and stressed out. Not knowing what else to do, she quickly makes up an excuse for her actions. Sue tells the teacher she couldn't finish her work because she had a

(continued)

Event	Description	Examples
	— Making up excuses or justifications. — Becoming angry and lashing out at others. — Adopting an "I don't care" attitude, trying to make it seem as if the unfinished work and inattentiveness are purposeful. — Changing the subject when confronted. — Blaming other people or circumstances for her lack of progress.	to her teacher, "Maybe I would listen if you ever figured out how to teach. All of you teachers think you are like gods or something, like we should hang on every word you say. This class doesn't help me at all. I could learn more from watching TV for an hour." really awful headache so she couldn't think straight, and she was afraid she'd get in trouble if she turned in any more unfinished work.

| Long-term consequences | If no intervention is made and the student continues to have problems with PTSD in the classroom, the following long-term effects are common:

— Significant knowledge gaps caused by missed material lead to continuing academic difficulty, even in the absence of memories and panic attacks.
— Low frustration tolerance, gives up easily.
— Compulsive lying.
— Chronic low self-esteem.
— At high risk for quitting school.
— At risk for chronic depression. | Amy continues to struggle with intrusive memories of getting abused by Jon. As time goes on, it gets harder and harder to understand the school work and harder to cover up the problem she has. Amy starts to feel like every time she goes to school her stupidity is thrown in her face. Amy finally gets tired of feeling like an idiot in school because she can't get Jon out of her head and she can't do most of the work. So, Amy calls it quits and just never goes back. | Sue's troubles in school just get worse and her self-esteem continues to drop. She tries her hardest in school because she believes she doesn't even deserve to go to school with her total lack of brains. She just goes so that her parents don't have to put up with her as much. |

For the Therapist

The *Survivor's Guide* was written specifically to educate adolescent females who have been sexually abused about how such abuse can affect people. Such education can be helpful in a number of ways. Victims of sexual abuse frequently blame themselves for not only the abuse but the effects of the abuse as well, which actively contributes to a negative self-image and low self-esteem. Providing education about the effects of sexual abuse helps survivors realize that some of their difficulties are a result of the abuse they experienced instead of some inherent personal flaws or faults, which they often believe is the case. Improved self-image is frequently the result of this learning process. Abuse victims many times believe that they are the only ones who feel the way they do or have had these types of difficulties, thinking they are "weird" or "crazy." Reading this book will help the survivor realize that her reactions and difficulties are normal for those who have been sexually abused and that she isn't alone. Young survivors sometimes find that they don't know any words with which to explain their abuse-related experiences to others. This book teaches some basic concepts and terms and gives clients the language and understanding to tell someone they've been "triggered" or talk about the "panic attack" they had last night.

The ideal usage of *The Survivor's Guide* is as an educational tool used in combination with therapy. The book can be used easily in individual and group therapy settings. When using the book in the adolescent abuse group, group members can read a chapter of the book each session and then discuss any situations in their own lives that relate to the information just read. Having group members read each chapter out loud as part of the group session encourages clients to ask questions and participate. It also helps ensure that any feelings or memories that come up as a result of the reading will be acknowledged and processed.

When using this book with adolescent clients, assigning a simple written assignment after each chapter based on the subject matter just read can help the client integrate the information just learned into her own experience. For example, after reading the section on triggers, having the client make a written list of her personal triggers and then rating each trigger on a numerical scale as to how upsetting each item is to her can help both therapist and client get a clearer picture of the types of triggers that this client is responding to.

The Survivor's Guide has been written so that each chapter can be read independently of the others. A youth doesn't have to read the whole book to understand any one section. This can be a helpful feature when working with an individual client. The therapist can assign only those sections that apply to her.

The examples peppered throughout the book frequently spark the client's interest and help the client to understand the concepts better, but they can also bring up memories of the client's own abuse. Clients should be told about this possibility and encouraged to discuss any memories that come up with the therapist. Therapists should be sensitive to the fact that for many survivors, the topics in this book may be hooked up to some very potent emotions and memories. Attempting to assimilate too much of the information too quickly could be overwhelming to clients and slow therapeutic progress. Thus the pacing of the reading is an important consideration and clients should be given permission to take it slow or take a break if needed.

Occasionally, youth workers may come across sexually abused teens who won't be getting therapy in the immediate future but are continuing to experience some effects of the abuse. For these teens, *The Survivor's Guide* is something they can read themselves that will help them understand and make sense of some of their behaviors and difficulties. A list of local crisis line and mental health agency phone numbers should be given to these teens along with the book, as well as instructions for her to take her time reading the book and to take a break and call for help if she begins to feel overwhelmed.

Parents, teachers, and professionals who deal with adolescent survivors may find this book useful in providing them with a better understanding of the adolescent survivor experience. This book may also be useful in providing education to certain adult clients. Abuse work causes regression in some clients, and the book's simplicity may allow it to be understood despite some regression.

Educating survivors about the effects of abuse can be helpful in improving self-esteem, communication, and understanding. It is the purpose of *The Survivor's Guide* to be helpful in providing this education in a format that is easy to read and understand.

About the Author

Sharice A. Lee is a counselor who has worked with adolescent survivors of sexual abuse for 6 years in a number of settings. She provides training for professionals and community groups on the effects of sexual abuse on the adolescent and continues to develop materials to assist adolescent survivors and the professionals who work with them. She lives in Washington State.